NATURAL WONDERS
OF THE
WORLD

Converting Distance Measurements to Metric Units

Kerri O'Donnell

Math
for the
REAL World™

Rosen Classroom Books & Materials
New York

Published in 2005 by The Rosen Publishing Group, Inc.
29 East 21st Street, New York, NY 10010

Book Design: Michael Tsanis

Photo Credits: Cover (Matterhorn, Ayers Rock), pp. 6, 10, 14, 21, 26, 29 © Corbis; cover (fish and coral),
pp. 5 (Rocky Mountains), 25 © Digital Vision; p. 5 (Monument Valley) © PhotoDisc; p. 9 © Buddy Mays/
Corbis; p. 13 © Art Wolfe/The Image Bank; p. 17 © Michele Westmoreland/The Image Bank; pp. 18–19,
22 © Punchstock; p. 22 (inset) © Darryl Torckler/Taxi; p. 30 © Charles and Josette Lenars/Corbis.

Library of Congress Cataloging-in-Publication Data

O'Donnell, Kerri, 1972-
   Natural wonders of the world : converting distance measurements to metric units / Kerri O'Donnell.
      v. cm.
   Includes index.
   Contents: So many wonders — The Grand Canyon — Mount Everest and K2 — The Matterhorn — Mighty
waterfalls — The wonders of Australia — The volcano of Paricutin — Meteor!
   ISBN 1-4042-2928-0 (lib. bdg.)
   ISBN 1-4042-5119-7 (pbk.)
   6-pack ISBN 1-4042-5120-0
   1. Metric system—Juvenile literature. 2. Natural monuments—Juvenile literature. [1. Metric system. 2.
Natural monuments. 3. Measurement.] I. Title.
   QC92.5.036 2004
   551.41—dc22
                                          2003028002

Manufactured in the United States of America

Contents

So Many Wonders

The world is full of many natural wonders. Tall mountains, deep gorges, crystal blue lakes, crashing waterfalls, and white-sand beaches are all examples of the great variety of Earth's landforms. Everywhere we look, we see Earth's natural features—even in our own backyards!

Some scientists use their knowledge of Earth's landforms to make lists of the "top" wonders of the world, and their opinions often vary. In this book, we will explore some of the world's most famous natural wonders and take a close look at what makes each of them **unique**.

To better understand these amazing places around the world, we will also take a look at 2 different systems of measurement: the inch-pound system and the metric system. The inch-pound system of weights and measures—also called the U.S. customary system—is used in the United States. This system measures length and distance using inches, feet, yards, and miles. Most other countries around the world use the metric system. The metric system measures length and distance in units called centimeters, meters, and kilometers.

These photographs show spectacular natural wonders found within the United States. The table shows some units of measurement used in the inch-pound system and the metric system.

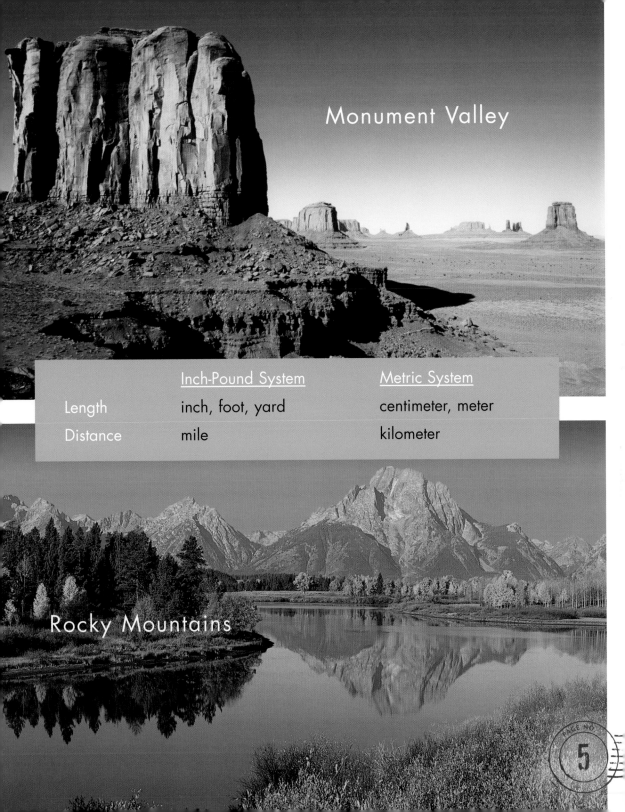

Monument Valley

	Inch-Pound System	Metric System
Length	inch, foot, yard	centimeter, meter
Distance	mile	kilometer

Rocky Mountains

Conversion Chart

If You Know:	Multiply by:	To Find:
miles	1.609	kilometers

Grand Canyon

The Grand Canyon

The Grand Canyon is located in the state of Arizona in the southwestern United States and is one of the most easily recognized natural wonders of the world. The Colorado River flows through the canyon and is responsible for the canyon's formation. Over a period of about 6 million years, the Colorado River cut through layers of rock in a process called **erosion**, forming the canyon we see today. In the canyon's deepest part, scientists have found rocks that are about 2 billion years old. They have also found plant and animal fossils that date back millions of years.

When measured using the inch-pound system, the Grand Canyon is about 1 mile deep. How deep is the canyon if you converted, or changed, that measurement into metric units? We can look at the **conversion** chart on page 6 to figure this out.

To convert miles to kilometers, we must first know how many kilometers are in 1 mile. There are 1.609 kilometers in 1 mile. We then multiply 1.609—which is called a **conversion factor**—by the number of miles (1).

$$\begin{array}{r} 1.609 \\ \times \quad 1 \text{ mile} \\ \hline 1.609 \text{ kilometers} \end{array}$$

The Grand Canyon is about 1.6 kilometers deep.

The Grand Canyon stretches for about 277 miles across northwestern Arizona. Let's convert that distance to kilometers.

Multiply 1.609 by the number of miles (277).

$$\begin{array}{r} 1.609 \\ \times \quad 277 \text{ miles} \\ \hline 11\ 263 \\ 112\ 63 \\ + \quad 321\ 8 \\ \hline 445.693 \text{ kilometers} \end{array}$$

Now round to the nearest kilometer. The Grand Canyon is about 446 kilometers long!

Because of the Grand Canyon's vast size, the climate is different depending on the elevation. The area near the bottom of the canyon, called the lower canyon, has an annual rainfall of about 9 inches. To express that measurement in metric units, we need to convert the inches to centimeters. We can use the chart on page 9 to make the conversion.

There are 2.54 centimeters in an inch. To convert inches to centimeters, we multiply 2.54 by the number of inches (9).

$$\begin{array}{r} 2.54 \\ \times \quad 9 \text{ inches} \\ \hline 22.86 \text{ centimeters} \end{array}$$

When rounded to the nearest centimeter, we see that the lower canyon gets about 23 centimeters of rain each year.

The highest part of the canyon's rim gets an average annual rainfall of about 26 inches. Let's convert that to metric units.

Multiply 2.54 by the number of inches (26).

$$\begin{array}{r} 2.54 \\ \times \quad 26 \text{ inches} \\ \hline 15\ 24 \\ +\ 50\ 8 \quad\ \\ \hline 66.04 \text{ centimeters} \end{array}$$

Now round to the nearest centimeter. The Grand Canyon's highest elevation gets about 66 centimeters of rain each year.

The Grand Canyon's different climates support a great variety of wildlife. Different kinds of pine trees grow along the canyon's rim. Cactuses also grow throughout the canyon. The canyon is home to animals such as bighorn sheep, mountain lions, elk, lizards, and snakes.

Conversion Chart

If You Know:	Multiply by:	To Find:
inches	2.54	centimeters

The cactuses in this picture of the lower canyon are called spinystars. In the summer months, spinystars grow pink or purple flowers.

Conversion Chart		
If You Know:	Multiply by:	To Find:
feet	.3048	meters

Mount Everest

As climbers scale Mount Everest, the air becomes "thinner," meaning there is less oxygen. This makes it difficult for people to take in enough oxygen when they breathe at higher elevations.

Mount Everest and K2

Mount Everest is the world's highest mountain. It is located in Asia on the border of Tibet and Nepal, and is part of a mountain system called the Himalayas. The mountain was named after Sir George Everest, a British **surveyor** who was stationed in nearby India in the 1800s.

There is some disagreement on the exact height of Mount Everest, but the official recorded height is 29,028 feet. We can use the conversion chart on page 10 to convert that to metric units.

To convert feet to meters, we multiply the number of feet (29,028) by .3048, since 1 foot is equal to .3048 meters.

$$
\begin{array}{r}
29{,}028 \text{ feet} \\
\times\ .3048 \\
\hline
23\ 2224 \\
116\ 112 \\
000\ 00 \\
+\ 8\ 708\ 4 \\
\hline
8{,}847.7344 \text{ meters}
\end{array}
$$

When rounded to the nearest meter, we find that Mount Everest is about 8,848 meters high!

Since the mid-1800s, many people have tried to climb Mount Everest, and many have died trying to reach the top. The climb is dangerous because of strong winds, freezing temperatures, **avalanches**, and the steepness of the mountain. In 1953, Sir Edmund Hillary and Tenzing Norgay were the first men to reach the mountain's **summit**.

The name "Himalaya" is the **Sanskrit** word for "house of snow." The Himalaya system is actually made up of several mountain ranges that run next to each other across southern Asia.

The Himalaya system extends about 1,500 miles from end to end. We can use the conversion chart on page 6 to convert that measurement to kilometers.

Multiply 1.609 by the number of miles (1,500).

```
        1.609
    x   1,500 miles
    ───────────────
        0 000
       00 00
      804 5
    + 1 609
    ───────────────
    2,413.500 kilometers
```

When we round this to the nearest kilometer, the answer is 2,414 kilometers.

K2, the second-highest mountain in the world, is also found in the Himalaya mountain system. This mountain—also called Dapsang or Mount Godwin Austen—can be found in one of the Himalaya's northwestern mountain ranges.

K2 is 28,250 feet high. Its peak is usually hidden by clouds. Some of the glaciers on its sides are about 40 miles long. Let's convert that measurement to kilometers.

Mount Godwin Austen was named for Englishman Henry Haversham Godwin Austen, who surveyed the mountain in the late 1850s. He referred to the mountain as "K2," since it was the second of the two highest peaks he surveyed in the Karakorum Range of the Himalayas.

Multiply 1.609 by the number of miles (40).

```
     1.609
 x    40 miles
 _____
   0 000
+ 64 36
 _____
  64.360 kilometers
```

When we round this to the nearest kilometer, the answer is 64 kilometers.

The Matterhorn

Many people have climbed the Matterhorn. The first person to reach the top was a man named Edward Whymper, who climbed the Matterhorn in 1865.

The Matterhorn

Though much smaller than Mount Everest and K2, a mountain called the Matterhorn is considered one of the world's most beautiful natural wonders. The mountain is located on the border between Italy and Switzerland and is part of the Pennine Alps, a mountain range known for its steep mountains and jagged peaks.

Although the base of the Matterhorn is located on the border between Italy and Switzerland, the mountain's peak is located in Switzerland. The Matterhorn got its name from its pyramid-shaped peak, which geologists call a "horn." The mountain's horn was formed by glaciers, which eroded the mountain's rock on both sides to create the pyramid shape. The Matterhorn rises to a height of 14,692 feet, and its upper peak is always covered with snow. We can use the conversion chart on page 10 to convert the Matterhorn's height to meters.

Multiply the number of feet (14,692) by .3048.

$$\begin{array}{r} 14{,}692 \text{ feet} \\ \times\ .3048 \\ \hline 11\ 7536 \\ 58\ 768 \\ 000\ 00 \\ +\ 4\ 407\ 6 \\ \hline 4{,}478.1216 \text{ meters} \end{array}$$

When we round this to the nearest meter, the answer is 4,478 meters.

Mighty Waterfalls

In southern Africa, you can find one of the most spectacular waterfalls in the world—Victoria Falls. Victoria Falls is located on the Zambezi River between the countries of Zimbabwe and Zambia. In 1855, David Livingstone—a Scottish explorer—named the waterfall for Britain's Queen Victoria.

The Zambezi River measures about 1 mile across at the falls. From the conversion we did on page 7, we can see that this is about 1.6 kilometers. At this location on the river, the water drops from a maximum height of about 355 feet into a deep, narrow gorge. Let's convert that measurement to meters using the conversion chart on page 10.

Multiply .3048 by the number of feet (355).

```
        .3048
      x 355 feet
      ─────────
      1 5240
     15 240
   + 91 44
   ──────────
   108.2040 meters
```

When we round this to the nearest meter, the answer is 108 meters.

Some of the most distinctive features of Victoria Falls are the roaring sound and the great amount of mist and spray created as the water crashes to the bottom of the gorge. People who live in the area call the waterfall "smoke that thunders" in their language.

Victoria Falls' great cloud of spray
can be seen from very far away.

Victoria Falls

Niagara Falls

Parts of the Niagara River are deeper than the height of the falls! The river is about 184 feet deep at the base of the falls. Use the conversion chart on page 10 to find out how many meters that is.

Another mighty waterfall is Niagara Falls, located on the Niagara River about halfway between Lake Erie and Lake Ontario. The Niagara River makes up part of the border between Canada and the United States.

Niagara Falls is actually made up of 2 different waterfalls—the American Falls (left) and the Horseshoe Falls (right). Most of the water flows over the Horseshoe Falls, which is located on the Canadian side of the border. The Niagara River rushes over the Horseshoe and American Falls into a deep gorge that extends beyond the falls for about 7 miles. Let's convert that measurement to kilometers using the conversion chart on page 6.

Multiply 1.609 by the number of miles (7).

1.609
x   7 miles
11.263 kilometers

When we round this to the nearest kilometer, the answer is 11 kilometers.

Each year, the Niagara Gorge gets longer. This is because the water continuously wears away at the rock as it rushes over the falls. In fact, Niagara Falls used to be located farther down the Niagara River. By the process of erosion over many years, the falls have moved about 7 miles (11 kilometers) back upstream, creating the Niagara Gorge.

The Wonders of Australia

We can travel to Australia to see more unique geological wonders. Ayers Rock, located in the desert of central Australia's Northern Territory, is the world's largest **monolith**. The rock rises up from the sandy plains that surround it to a height of 1,142 feet. Let's use the conversion chart on page 10 to convert that measurement to metric units.

Multiply the number of feet (1,142) by .3048.

```
    1,142 feet
  x .3048
  _____
    9136
  4 568
000 00
+ 342 6
_____
348.0816 meters
```

When we round this to the nearest meter, the answer is 348 meters.

Like many of the world's natural wonders, Ayers Rock was formed by erosion. Scientists believe this erosion may have started as early as 138 million years ago. The rock is made of sandstone, which glows with a reddish color at different times of the day depending on the light. Aborigines—the native people of Australia—call Ayers Rock "Uluru," which means "great pebble." In 1878, an explorer named William Gosse named the rock after Henry Ayers, who was the prime minister of South Australia at the time.

The distance around the rock's base is about 5.5 miles. Let's convert that to kilometers using the conversion chart on page 6.

Multiply 1.609 by the number of miles (5.5).

$$
\begin{array}{r}
1.609 \\
\times \quad 5.5 \text{ miles} \\
\hline
8045 \\
+ \ 8\ 045 \\
\hline
8.8495 \text{ kilometers}
\end{array}
$$

When we round this to the nearest kilometer, the answer is 9 kilometers.

Ayers Rock

Ayers Rock is about 2 miles long and about 1.5 miles wide. Use the conversion information above to find those distances in kilometers.

Conversion Chart		
If You Know:	Multiply by:	To Find:
feet	30.48	centimeters

polyps

Great Barrier Reef

Australia is also home to the world's largest coral reef, called the Great Barrier Reef. The Great Barrier Reef is actually a chain of many different reefs in the Pacific Ocean. These reefs extend along Australia's northeastern coast for about 1,250 miles. Let's use the conversion chart on page 6 to convert that to kilometers.

Multiply the number of miles (1,250) by 1.609.

```
      1,250 miles
    x  1.609
     11 250
     00 00
     750 0
   + 1 250
    2,011.25  kilometers
```

When we round this to the nearest kilometer, the answer is 2,011 kilometers.

The Great Barrier Reef's coral is formed by sea animals called **polyps**. When the polyps die, their skeletons form a rock called limestone. New, living polyps attach themselves to the limestone left by the dead polyps. When those living polyps die, their skeletons also form limestone and the coral grows larger. Some polyps are very small, measuring just 1 inch. If we look at the conversion chart on page 9, we see that 1 inch converts to 2.54 centimeters.

Others polyps are much larger, and can grow to be 1 foot long. Let's use the conversion chart on page 22 to convert that to centimeters.

To convert feet to centimeters, we multiply 30.48 by the number of feet (1), since there are 30.48 centimeters in 1 foot.

```
    30.48
  x      1 foot
    30.48 centimeters
```

When rounded to the nearest centimeter, we see that the larger polyps can be about 30 centimeters long.

Like most coral reefs around the world, the Great Barrier Reef lies just under or just above the ocean's surface in warm, shallow water. Scientists believe the Great Barrier Reef has about 400 different kinds of polyps! Polyps come in many different colors, such as red, yellow, tan, green, blue, and purple. The polyps that make up the Great Barrier Reef are what give the reef its vibrant colors.

The reef also gets its amazing colors from the many fish and other sea animals that live there. Fish, sea worms, shrimp, crabs, clams, and snails all make their homes in the reef near the ocean's surface. Many tourists visit Australia each year to go diving around the reef and to see the vast array of ocean life it supports. At its closest point, the reef lies about 10 miles off Australia's coast. At its furthest point, the reef lies more than 100 miles off the coast.

We can use simple multiplication to quickly convert these distances to kilometers. Since we know that 1 mile is equal to 1.609 kilometers, we can round that decimal to 1.6 to simplify our calculations. If we multiply 10 miles by 1.6 kilometers, we simply move the decimal point one space to the right to get the answer: 16 kilometers. What do we get if we multiply 100 miles by 1.6? Just move the decimal place two places to the right for the answer.

10 miles x 1.6 = 16 kilometers	100 miles x 1.6 = 160 kilometers
1.6 → 1.6.	1.6 → 16. → 160.

Coral reefs make up only about 1% of the ocean floor, but are home to nearly 25% of the plants and animals living in the oceans.

Multiply .3048 by the number of feet (150).

```
    .3048
  x 150 feet
 ----------
    0000
  15 240
+ 30 48
 ----------
  45.7200 meters
```

When we round this to the nearest meter, the answer is 46 meters.

Paricutin volcano

The Volcano of Paricutin

The youngest volcano in the Western Hemisphere, called Paricutin (puh-REE-kuh-teen), can be found in southwestern Mexico. The volcano was named after the village of Paricutin, which was destroyed by the volcano's first eruption in 1943.

One of the most unique things about this natural wonder is the way it was formed. Unlike most of the world's natural geologic wonders, Paricutin did not take millions or even thousands of years to form. It took only a few years, making it a very interesting place for scientists to study.

On February 20, 1943, a crack appeared in the ground of a Mexican cornfield while a farmer and a few other witnesses watched in amazement. The ground shook, and within moments volcanic ash began to erupt from the crack. The ground swelled as the farmer watched, forming a hill that was about 7 feet high. The people in the area quickly fled. Within 24 hours, the volcanic cone had reached a height of about 150 feet! We can use the conversion chart on page 10 to convert this to meters.

On the second night of Paricutin's eruption, people in the area reported that volcanic material shot up about 1,000 feet into the air. Use the same conversion factor as the one used on page 26 to figure out how many meters that is.

By the end of that week, the volcanic cone had reached a height of about 328 feet! Let's figure out the metric equivalent in meters.

Multiply .3048 by the number of feet (328).

$$
\begin{array}{r}
.3048 \\
\times\ 328\ \text{feet} \\
\hline
2\ 4384 \\
6\ 096 \\
+\ 91\ 44 \\
\hline
99.9744\ \text{meters}
\end{array}
$$

When we round this to the nearest meter, the answer is 100 meters.

Lava from the volcano covered the village's cornfields. Within days, it had destroyed the village of Paricutin and several surrounding villages. Two months later, the volcanic cone stood at 1,000 feet. By rounding the conversion factor above to .30 and multiplying by 1,000, we can estimate that height in meters.

1,000 feet x .30 = 300 meters

.30 ➙ 3.0 ➙ 3 0.0 ➙ 30.0.

Paricutin's activity gradually decreased and finally stopped in 1952. In just 9 years, the volcano had reached a height of 1,345 feet! See if you can convert that measurement to meters.

Paricutin's volcanic material covers an area of about 19 square miles. Using the metric system, this area measurement would be given in square kilometers. Use the conversion chart on page 29 to figure out how many square kilometers are covered by Paricutin's **volcanic debris**.

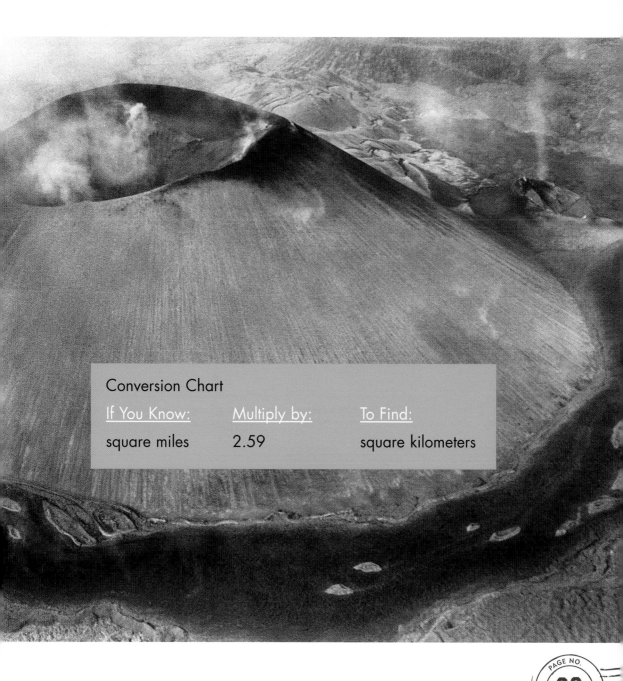

Conversion Chart

If You Know:	Multiply by:	To Find:
square miles	2.59	square kilometers

Meteor!

Another geologic landform was created suddenly about 50,000 years ago when a **meteorite** hit Earth in the area that is today known as Winslow, Arizona. The force of the meteorite hitting Earth's surface left a huge circular **depression** on the land, forming Meteor Crater. The meteorite went so deep upon impact that it has never been found. However, the crater it left in Earth's surface has remained nearly the same for 50,000 years.

Meteor Crater is 570 feet deep and about 4,180 feet wide. Now you can use what you know about metric conversions to express those measurements in meters!

Meteor Crater

Glossary

avalanche (AA-vuh-lanch) A large mass of snow or rocks that suddenly slides or falls down the side of a mountain.

conversion (kuhn-VUHR-zhun) The act of changing something into a different form.

conversion factor (kuhn-VUHR-zhun FAK-tuhr) A number that when multiplied by a given number of units expresses the equivalent number of units in a different measurement system.

depression (dih-PREH-shun) A low, hollow place.

erosion (ih-ROH-zhun) The process of being gradually worn away.

meteorite (MEE-tee-uh-rite) A mass of stone and metal that falls from outer space to a planet or moon.

monolith (MAH-nuh-lith) A very large stone.

polyp (PAH-luhp) A small water animal.

Sanskrit (SAN-skrit) The ancient written language of India.

summit (SUH-muht) The highest point of a mountain.

surveyor (suhr-VAY-uhr) One who is trained to measure land with mathematics and special tools.

unique (yoo-NEEK) Having traits that are like no other thing or person.

volcanic debris (vahl-KA-nik duh-BREE) Layers of cooled, hardened lava and ash.

Index